STORIES OF THE TITANS

Mythology Stories for Kids
Children's Folk Tales & Myths

BABY PROFESSOR
EDUCATION KIDS

Speedy Publishing LLC

40 E. Main St. #1156

Newark, DE 19711

www.speedypublishing.com

Copyright 2017

All Rights reserved. No part of this book may be reproduced or used in any way or form or by any means whether electronic or mechanical, this means that you cannot record or photocopy any material ideas or tips that are provided in this book

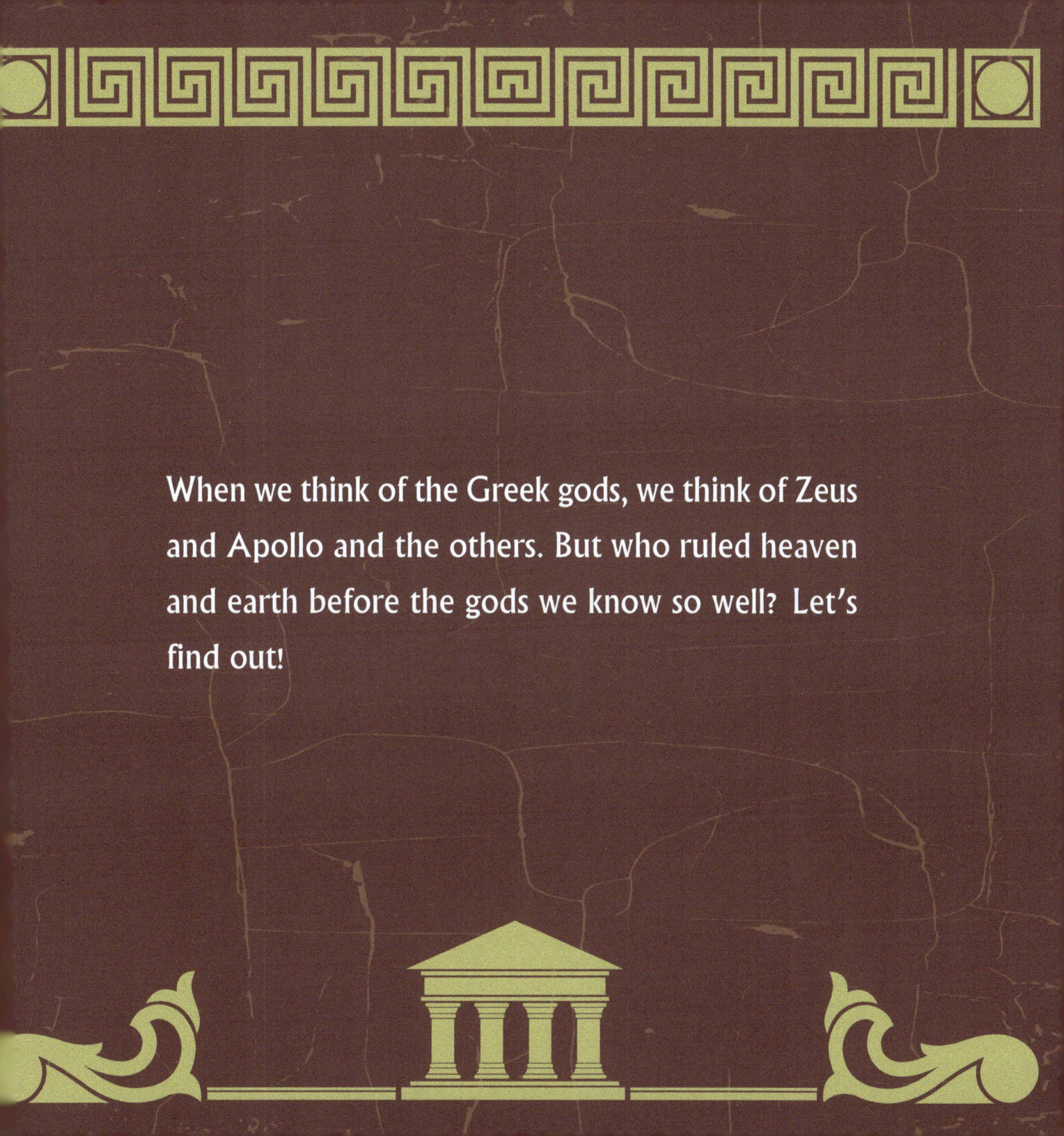

When we think of the Greek gods, we think of Zeus and Apollo and the others. But who ruled heaven and earth before the gods we know so well? Let's find out!

WHO WERE THE TITANS?

Before the gods of Mount Olympus, Zeus and the others, there were the Titans. The Titans were the children of Earth (Gaea) and Heaven (Uranus). They were huge, like giants, and incredibly strong. Their home was Mount Othrys in Greece.

CYCLOPES

Gaea and Uranus first had children who were less like humans and more like monsters. These included the Cyclopes, giants with a single eye each and huge monsters who had hundreds of hands. In the classic story The Odyssey, Odysseus has to save his crew from Polyphemus, a Cyclops. (Read more about this in the Baby Professor book The Adventures of Odysseus.)

Uranus was afraid of these monstrous children, and sent them into deep dungeons and caves in the Earth. Then he and Gaea had twelve children who were as beautiful and wonderful as the first children had been terrible and scary.

The brothers were:

CRONOS

He was the god of time, and was leader of the Titans although he was the youngest of the first generation.

HYPERION

He was the god of light. One of his sons was Helios, the god of the Sun and his daughter Selene drove the chariot of the Moon across the night sky.

HELIOS

COEUS

He was the god of wisdom and of knowledge of the stars.

CRIUS

He controlled the constellations in the night sky.

IAPETUS

He was the god of immortality, and his children include some of the most powerful Titans, like Prometheus and Atlas.

OCEANUS

He was the oldest Titan, and controlled the sea.

RHEA

She was the wife of her brother Cronus, and queen of the Titans. She controlled fertility and motherhood.

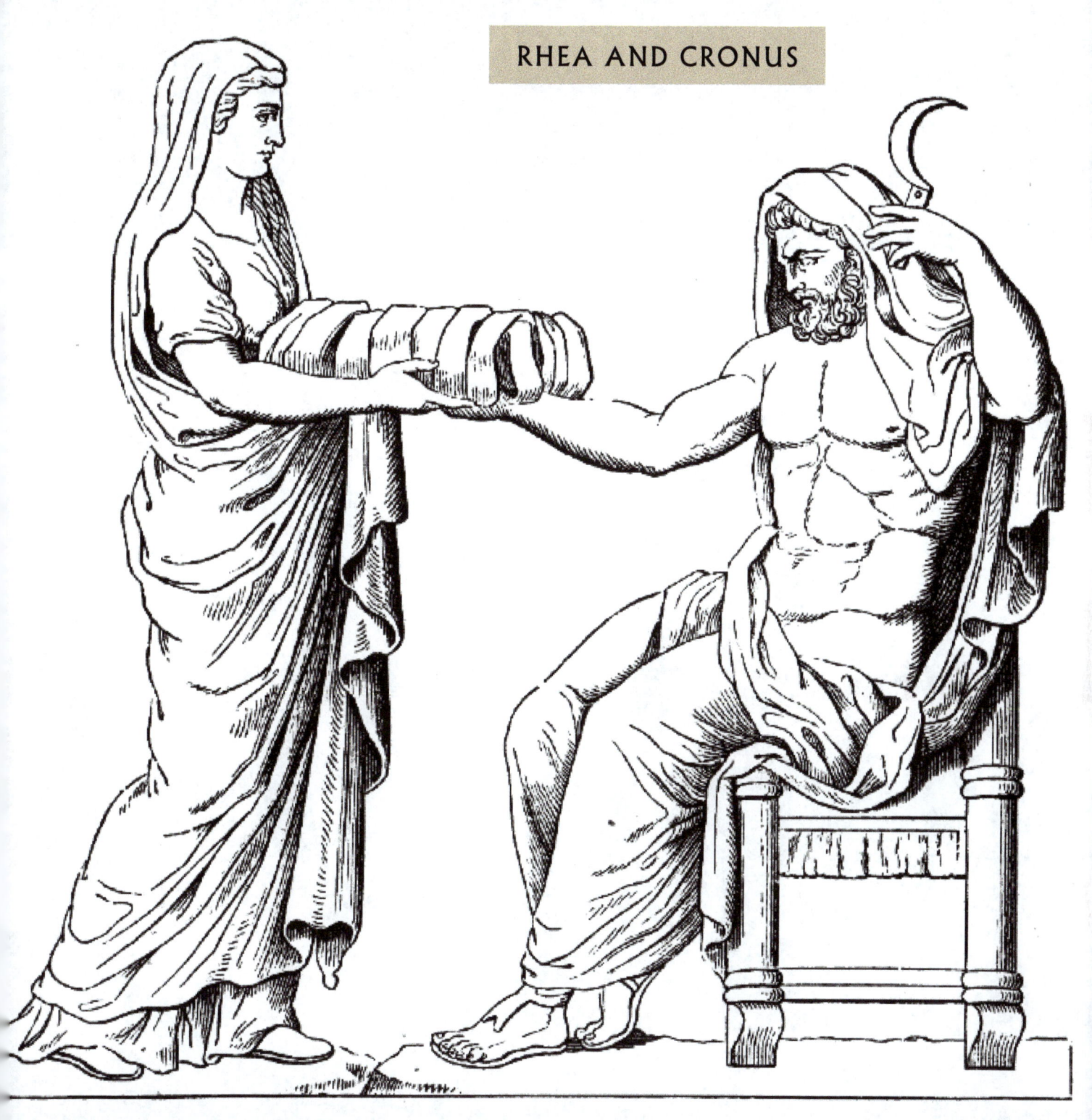
RHEA AND CRONUS

TETHYS

She was married to her brother Oceanus and shared control of the creatures of the sea with him.

THEIA

She was married to her brother Hyperion and was the goddess of all shining and glittering things, and of both sight and foresight (the ability to see the future).

PHOEBE

She was the goddess of light, of memory, of insights, and of predictions and oracles.

THEMIS

She was the goddess
of order and justice.

Some of the children of the Titans also figured in Greek myths.

The Fates, who weave the fabric of people's lives, were the children of Themis.

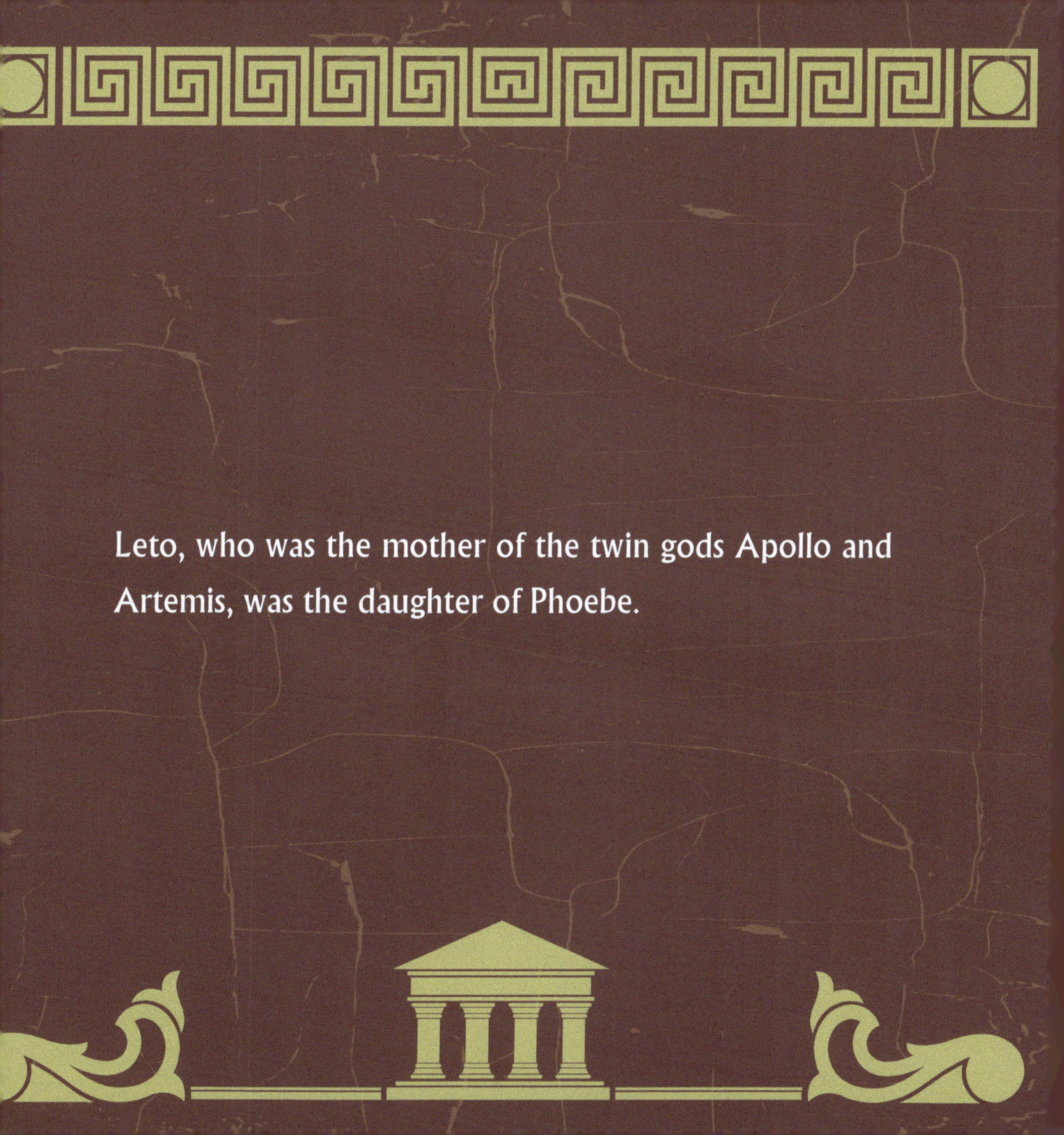

Leto, who was the mother of the twin gods Apollo and Artemis, was the daughter of Phoebe.

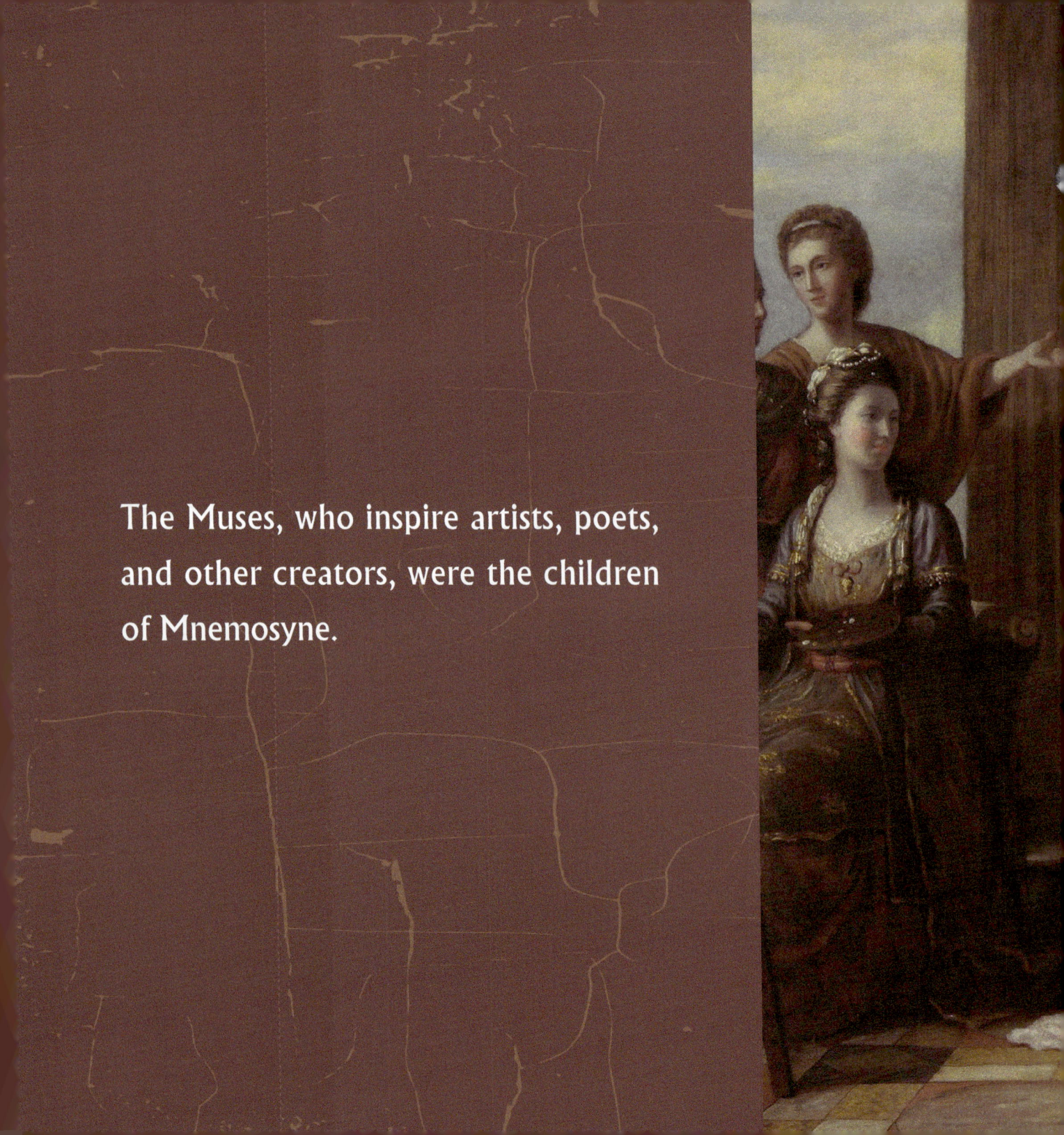

The Muses, who inspire artists, poets, and other creators, were the children of Mnemosyne.

THE RISE OF THE TITANS

The Titans rebelled against their parents, and fought to overthrow them. Rhea made a sickle, a kind of curved knife mainly used for harvesting. She gave this weapon to Cronos, who attacked his father Uranus with it and defeated him.

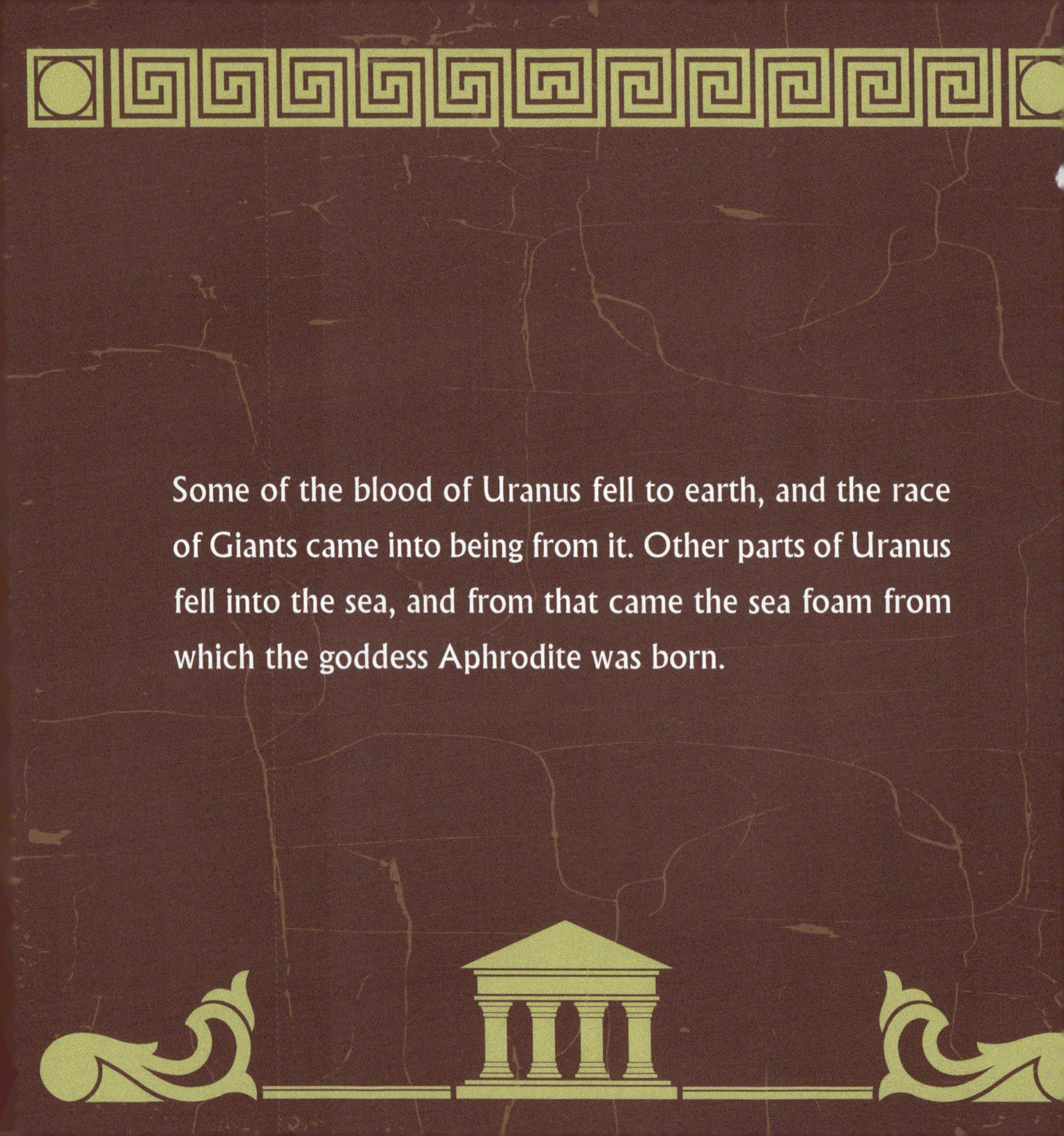

Some of the blood of Uranus fell to earth, and the race of Giants came into being from it. Other parts of Uranus fell into the sea, and from that came the sea foam from which the goddess Aphrodite was born.

APHRODITE

In Greek myths, the time of the Titans was a golden age for people. It was a time of learning, invention, and exploration. The Titans ruled the heavens and the Earth, but did not have much to do with humans. That would change under the Olympian gods, who interfered in human history a lot! You can read about them in the Baby Professor book The Greek Gods and Heroes.

HOW THE TITANS FELL

Cronos, the leader of the Titans, replaced his father Uranus as king of all things. But he heard a prophecy that, as he had defeated his father, his own children would defeat him. So he developed a desperate plan to prevent the prophecy coming true. As each of his children was born, he swallowed the baby! In this way he swallowed Hestia, Hera, Hades, Demeter, Poseidon, and other future Olympian gods.

CRONOS

CRETE, GREECE

There were two problems with this plan. First, Cronos could not digest his children, so they stayed inside him and grew to adulthood. Second, Rhea, his sister and wife, did not agree with the plan. She took one child, her son Zeus, and hid him away on the island of Crete. In his place, she wrapped a large rock in a blanket and Cronos swallowed that!

On Crete, Zeus grew up in secret until he was powerful enough to face his father. But, according to one story, Rhea made a plan that meant that Zeus did not have to fight his father. Rhea created a great banquet for Cronos of all his favorite foods (except for children!). In the feast were two strong potions. The first made Kronos so sick that he vomited up everything in his stomach—including all his children, who were now adults and ready to stand up to him! The second potion put Cronos in a profound sleep.

ZEUS

ZEUS

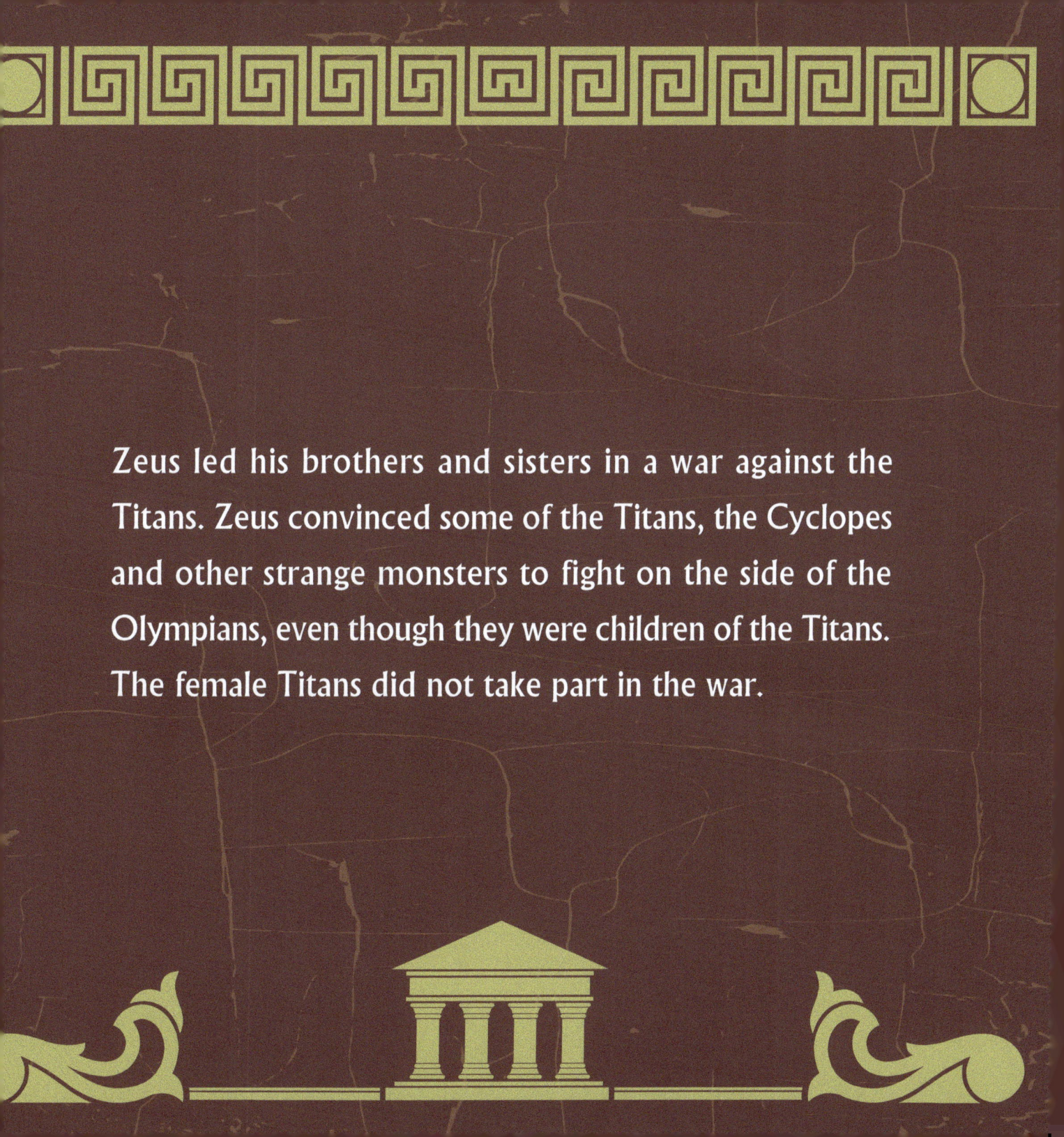

Zeus led his brothers and sisters in a war against the Titans. Zeus convinced some of the Titans, the Cyclopes and other strange monsters to fight on the side of the Olympians, even though they were children of the Titans. The female Titans did not take part in the war.

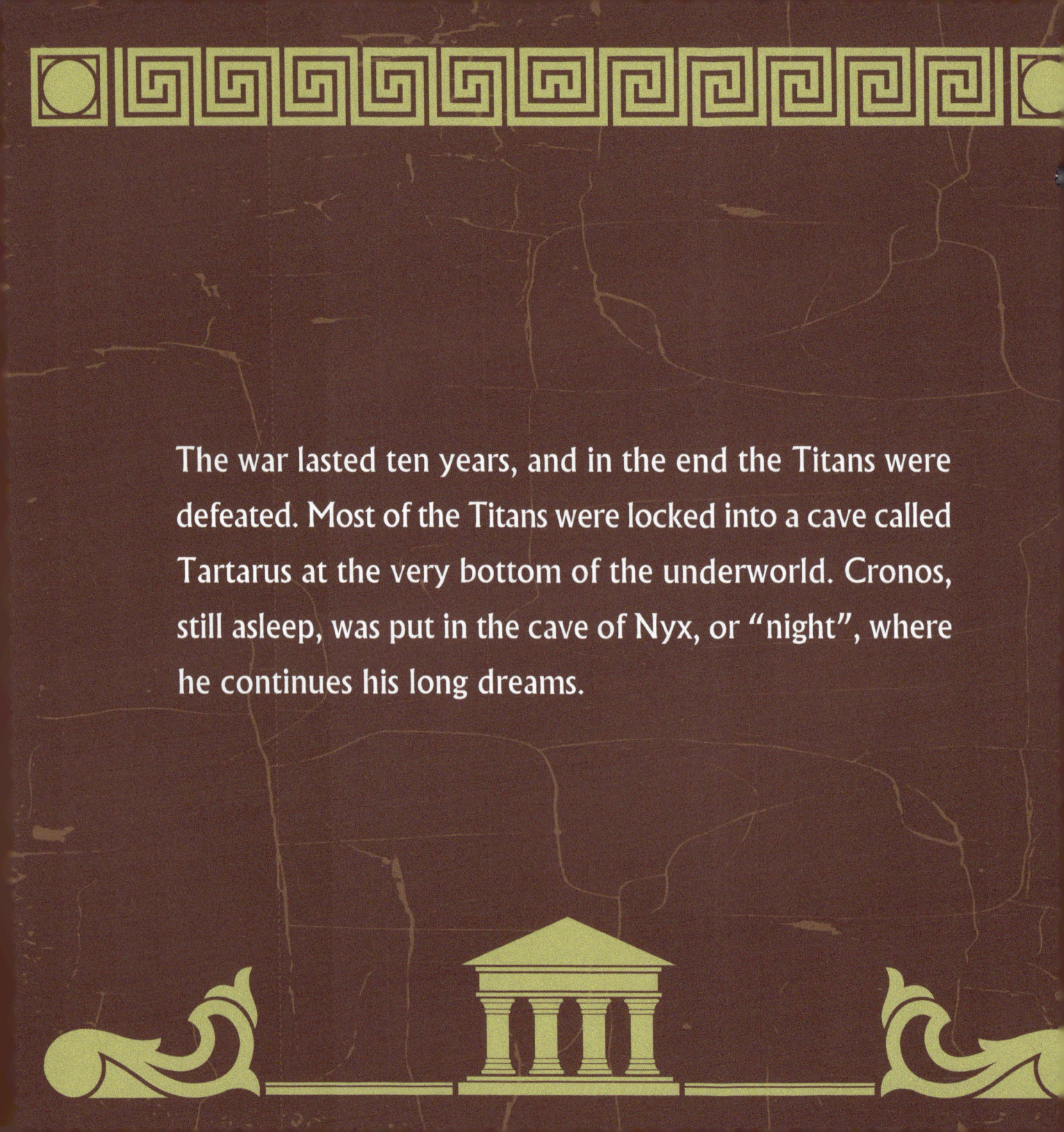

The war lasted ten years, and in the end the Titans were defeated. Most of the Titans were locked into a cave called Tartarus at the very bottom of the underworld. Cronos, still asleep, was put in the cave of Nyx, or "night", where he continues his long dreams.

UNDERWORLD

APOLLO

Some of the Titans had fought on the Olympian side, and were allowed to continue in freedom. Helios, son of the Titan Hyperion, was allowed to continue driving the Sun across the sky until, eventually, Apollo took over that task.

Zeus and his brothers Poseidon and Hades divided up the universe that Cronos had once ruled. Zeus became the sky god and the ruler of all the gods. Poseidon became the ruler of the sea, replacing Oceanus, and Hades became the god of the underworld. The three Olympians shared control of the world of people.

POSEIDON

ATLAS

MYTHS INVOLVING THE TITANS

Atlas, a son of the Titans who had helped lead the Titan side in the war, was condemned to carry the sky on his shoulders. He was made to stand at the far west of the world and keep the sky and the Earth apart. Hercules had to take over the job at one point, and had to trick Atlas into taking it back! Read about that adventure in the Baby Professor book Who was Hercules?

Another story about the Titans involved Dionysus, the god of fertility, wine, and creativity. In this story, Zeus has decided he would like to retire as chief god, and chooses the child Dionysus to replace him. The Titans who were not locked in Tartarus decide that if they could kill Dionysus they could recapture the power that they had once had under Cronos. They trick Dionysus with toys and then take him away, cook, and eat him. But Athena keeps the heart of Dionysus inside a doll where the Titans do not think to look for it. After Zeus kills the rebel Titans in a fury, Athena recreates Dionysus, starting from just his heart.

DIONYSUS

PROMETHEUS

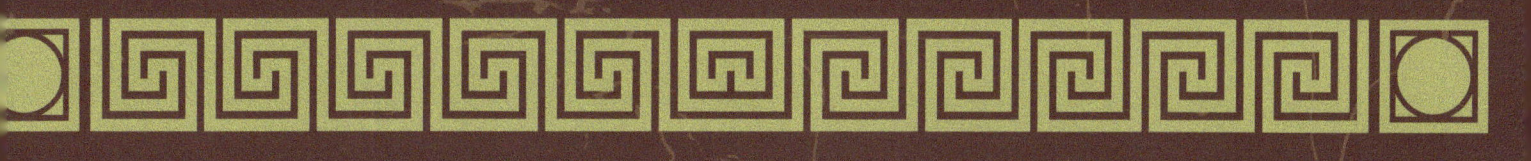

A third great myth involves Prometheus, a child of the Titan Iapetus. In some myths Prometheus creates people from clay; but in most of the stories he brings culture to people. He steals fire from Zeus and gives it to people so they can cook their food instead of eating it raw, like animals. This begins to set them apart from other creatures on Earth. Having fire also lets people make sacrifices, which means they can speak to the gods to ask them for help or to thank them for good things. This in some way takes people part-way to being gods!

Zeus gets upset with Prometheus, as he made these gifts to people without getting permission. Zeus chains Prometheus to the top of a mountain, and every day eagles come to dine on him, eating his liver. Every night Prometheus' liver grows back so the eagles can torture him again. Finally, Hercules frees Prometheus from his eternal punishment.

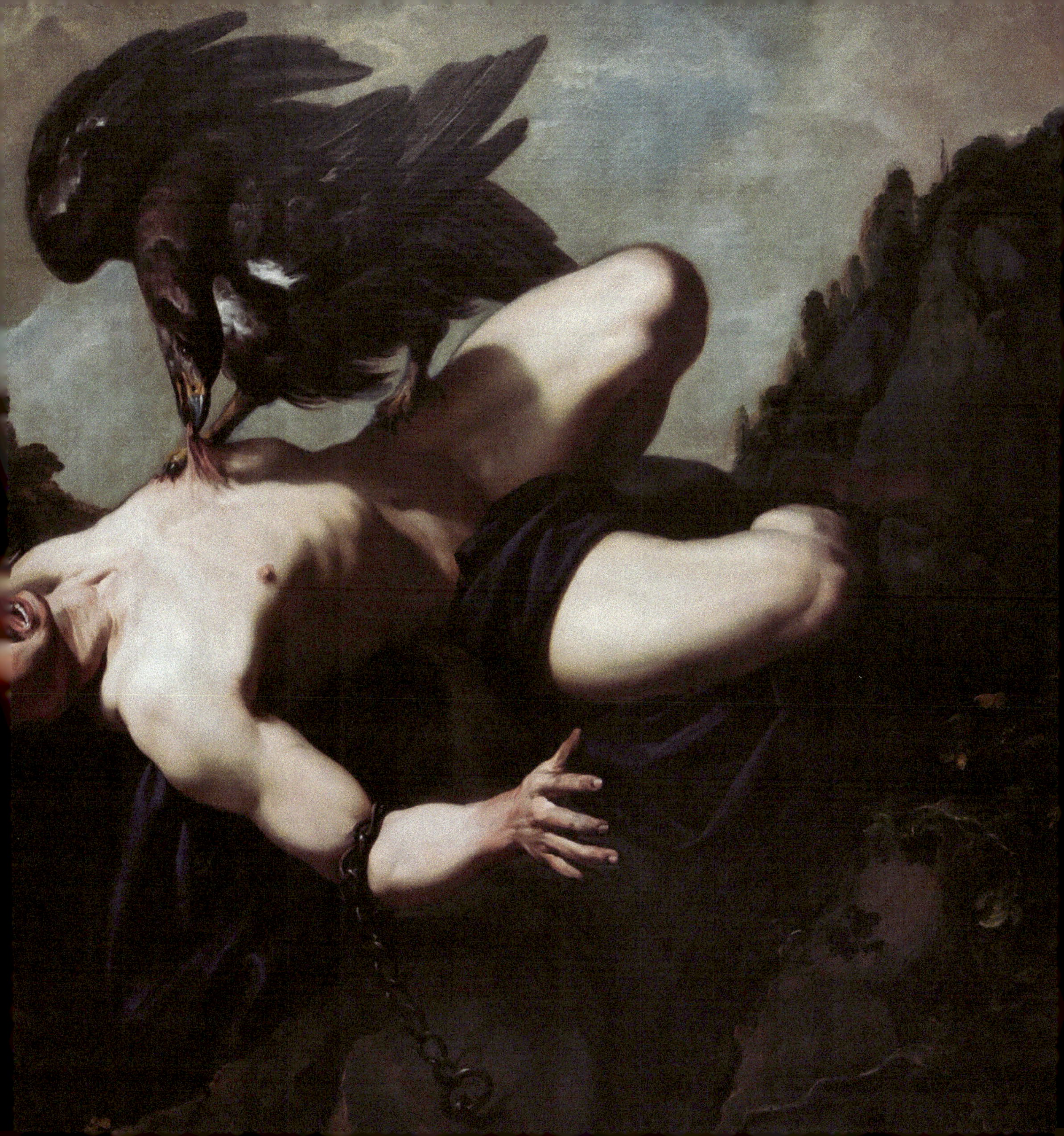

TEMPLE OF OLYMPIAN ZEUS

THE MAKING OF PEOPLE

Many Greeks believed that the first people came from the bodies of the defeated Titans. We inherit their power and wildness, but also the ability to dream and to create because the Titans had eaten Dionysus. As well, because of gifts from Prometheus and the Olympian gods we also have intelligence, creative and mechanical skills, and the ability to love and to be loyal. We are something new and wonderful in the world!

Read about other myths of heroes and gods from around the world in Baby Professor books like Apollo's Deadly Bow and Arrow, The Aztecs' Many Gods, and The World is Full of Spirits – Native American Religion, Mythology, and Legends.

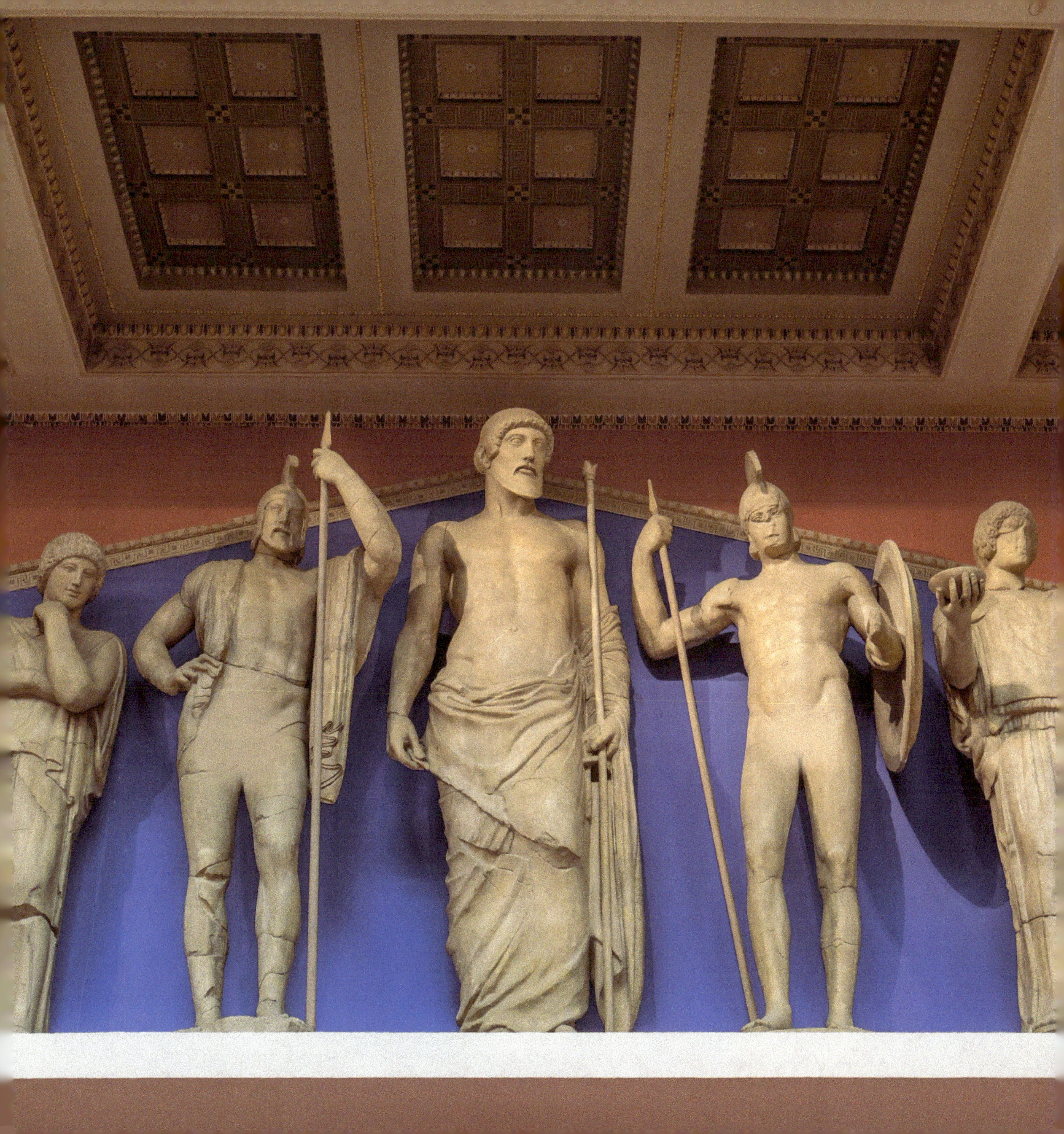

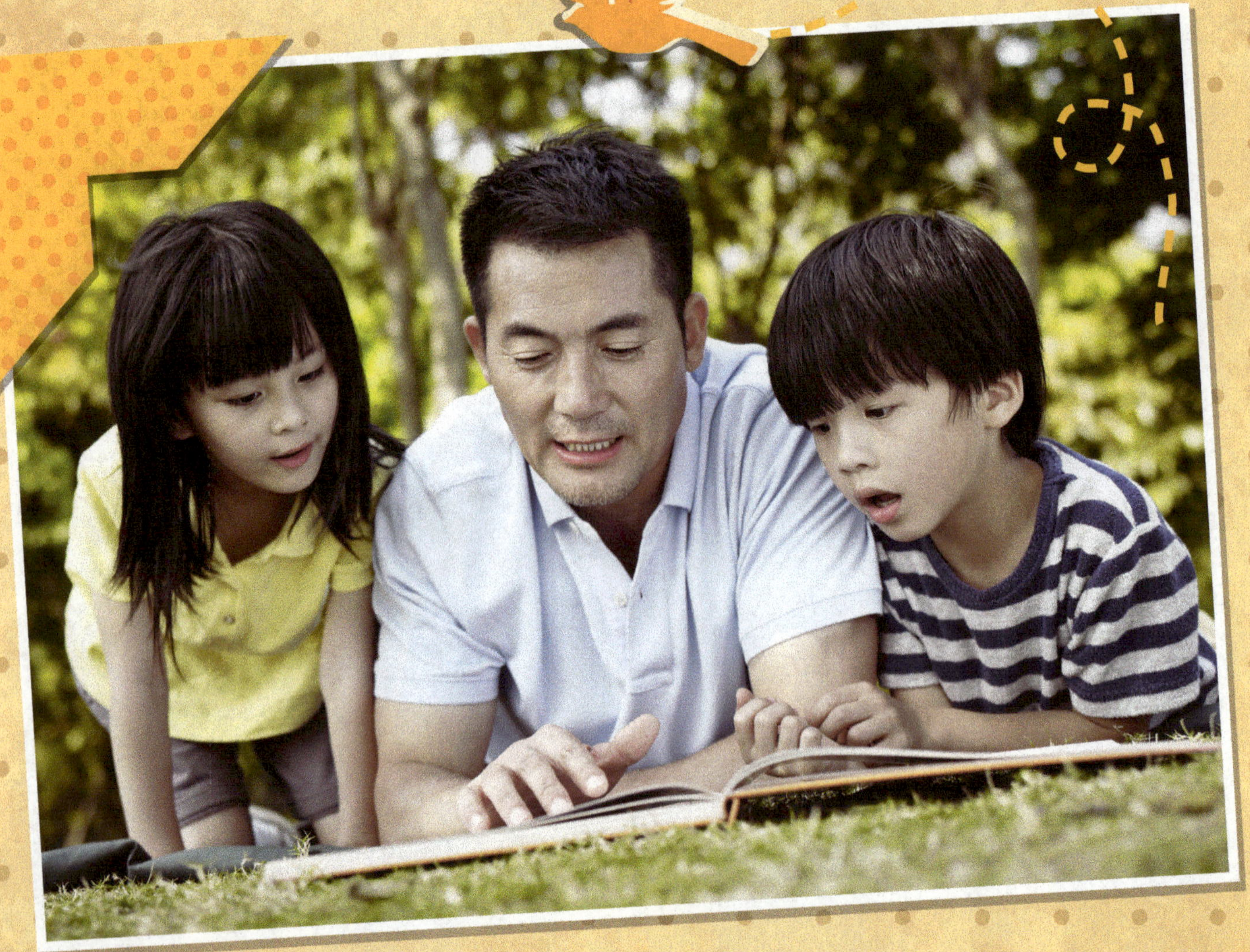

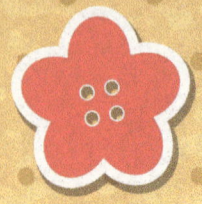

Visit

BABY PROFESSOR
EDUCATION KIDS

www.BabyProfessorBooks.com

to download Free Baby Professor eBooks
and view our catalog of new and exciting
Children's Books

Milton Keynes UK
Ingram Content Group UK Ltd.
UKHW051217040924
447642UK00021B/116